Build

Business

Value

F. Scott Pfeiffer

Business Management Consultant
Strategy Business Consulting, LLC

B.

BlissPoint Press
San Jose, CA

Published by BlissPoint Press.

www.BlissPointPress.com

This is the first edition. If you would like to make suggestions or comments for a second edition, please send an email to strategybusinessconsulting@gmail.com.

Build

Business

Value

Take Action Now

Increase the Value of your Business

Get the Most when You Sell

For Henry and Claire

Preface

For many entrepreneurs, the goal of starting and building a successful business is to exit that business with a liquidity event. To say that in English - you want to sell your company and make some money. You are not just operating a business - you are building an asset.

Much of the advice you will receive along the way, however, is good advice for operating the company and taking as much cash out as possible, mostly by reducing the tax burden - but it is not good advice for building the asset. In fact, much of the time you will be balancing your decisions between current operations and asset building.

This book was written to give you advice on the asset-building part of managing your company. Some of this advice you won't get from your current advisors if they are focused on this year, and some of it will be contrary to their advice. You should not always take my advice and ignore theirs: as I said, you must find a balance between current cash and tax reduction versus building business value. Not everyone will, or should, strike the same balance.

One final, and important, point: Many business owners will operate their company for years to pay the least taxes and take out as much cash as they can, and then want to sell the business and think that this can be done immediately. Not so. It takes years of careful planning and operating the company to build value before you can usually exit with a good sale. Sure, sometimes your special sauce is so special someone will snap you up just to get access to your IP, or your customer list, or a contract or regulatory license you have, but in general, building a business that has value is the work of years.

That is why, if you want to sell later, you must begin building business value now.

Scott Pfeiffer
Greenville, SC

About This Book

This book will give you an overview of steps you can begin taking today to build the valuable business you want.

The book does not tell you how to make and sell your product or how to deliver your service - I assume you know how to do all that. The bedrock on which business value rests is that of an excellent product or service, competently delivered, and having a competitive advantage in price, service, or quality.

Instead, this book tells you how to make decisions about the business that will enhance long term value, in lieu of reducing taxes and taking out cash.

There is nothing wrong with operating your business with a goal of reducing taxes and taking out as much cash as you can along the way. But understand that operating the business in this manner will not increase the value of the business over time as much, and if you want to sell the business later, the value will be much lower.

You can take the value out now,
or build value for later, but it's
hard to do both.

In the Appendices, I include an Accounting for Entrepreneurs section that lays out the basic financial reports and analyses you may encounter and gives you some very basic tips for interpreting those documents. Any entrepreneur who is intent on building value needs to be conversant with these financial reports and analysis tools.

It is important that you understand how to read these financial reports and basic analyses and understand how others - bankers and buyers - will read them. These financial statements are the lenses through which a lender or acquirer will view your business. By understanding them you can see how the steps in this book will affect value, you can monitor your business's progress along the way, and you can better evaluate the advice your professionals will give you along the way.

Table of Contents

One

Show Net Profit

Run a Profitable Company

You would think it goes without saying: run your business to make a profit. But not showing annual profits is one of the biggest mistakes small business owners make.

Your tax adviser may well tell you that your goal is to do just the opposite: to maximize deductions in order to have little or no end-of-year taxable income. After all, why pay tax when you don't have to? And while this may be sound short-term cash flow advice, it will not help you sell for value when the time comes.

Let me stop here and say, you don't have to operate your small business with an end goal of building its value and selling it some day. Operating a business to make money now and then shut it down, or hand it off to your kids, or sell it for just a little at the end – those are all perfectly acceptable strategies you may wish to employ. If you are operating your business this way, minimizing current taxes may be an excellent way to implement that strategy.

But this book is about growing business value with an eye to eventually selling your business at a good multiple. An "exit."

And if you are about building business value, showing increasing annual profit is an absolute must.

Small business valuations are driven by a net present value of the business's profits. Often, the valuation will be based on the company's EBITDA – which is simply its net profit (earnings) with payments for interest, taxes, depreciation and amortization added back to the bottom line.[1]

Most valuators and purchasers will use a formula that takes into account the last three, or even five, years of a business's EBITDA. Showing a strong, growing EBITDA will result in a higher valuation than a small EBITDA, or one that goes up and down from year to year. This is because a yo-yo ing EBITDA either implies risk or deception. Let me explain:

If I am to buy a business, and I assign a value for that business, I want some reasonable certainty that the business will either continue as it is or will grow. If your business makes $1 million per year in profits, and I pay you $5 million for the business, I want to be reasonably certain that the business will continue to make $1 million per year, or more. If your profits go wildly up and down each year, then I am uncertain how much the business will continue to make in the future, and I will lower my estimate of the business's value in order to minimize my risk.

---

[1] By "bottom line" I am referring to the number at the bottom of a profit and loss statement, one of the financial statements people use to analyze a business. I explain these financial statements and the terms used to describe them more completely in the Appendix.

I'll also consider that you may be achieving the highly profitable years by manipulating invoicing and cash flow to artificially inflate one year at the expense of the years on each side. This will make a savvy buyer look closely at your invoicing and check depositing and may result in a loss of trust as to the rest of your numbers and assertions, which could be fatal to the deal. At a minimum, the buyer is going to average the profits over several years, and you won't likely get a multiple based on your highest profits.

I should explain here the word "multiple" because you will hear it quite a bit when it comes to valuing businesses. A multiple (sometimes people will call it a "turn") is simply the number by which you multiply profits (or EBITDA) to get a value for the business. If your company has $1 million in EBITDA, and someone tells you it is worth a "3x multiple" or "3 turns", then they are saying your business is worth $3 million. How many multiples or turns on profits a business gets is dependent on a lot of factors, including:

- The type of business and industry
- The level of profits (businesses with $10 million in profits get higher multiples than businesses with $1 million in profits, generally)
- The age of the business
- Growth over time
- Confidence in the business's financial records

- Professionalism of the business and staff
- Intellectual property
- Recurring revenue
- Contracts
- Etc., etc. etc.

But no matter how many turns your business will generate, the base number will likely be some form of net profits or EBITDA. That's why showing strong, growing, annual net profit is the foundation of growing business value. And, because the buyer is going to look back three or even five years, it is a step to begin to take today. You can't just show one year's profit when you are ready to sell and expect to get good value.

People will tell you that you can have the best of both worlds. That you can show little or no profit year over year, and yet show value when it is time to sell, through the magic of "recasting." It is true that a valuator will often recast your financial statements to show more income than you reported to the IRS (or less, as the case may be). How?

The financial evaluation of your business during the "due diligence" period of the purchase transaction will include the buyer looking over all the deductions you took from gross revenue to reach net profit. They will also look closely at items you capitalized and amortized or depreciated rather than deducted. They are trying to determine the "real" net earnings of the business in order to be more confident in their valuation.

If you deducted items that really were not business expenses – like your daughter's horseback riding lessons, or your trip to Hawaii that had only a thin business connection, or all the meals or entertainment or marketing you deducted that were really unnecessary for the continuing success of the business – they will reconsider those items as compensation to you, the owner(s). Then they will add up all the compensation the owners took, including salaries and all these "expenses," and decide if that compensation was more than the new buyer would have to pay to replace the labor you gave the business. If so, the valuator will increase the net profit by the amount your revised "compensation" exceeds the value of the labor. If not, if you underpaid yourself to try and increase profits[2], they will determine the reasonable replacement value of your services and deduct that from your reported net profits.

There is, however, a catch: all this "recasting" is not the magic solution it seems to be. Every item that is recast increases the amount of time spent in due diligence, leads to additional questions and examinations, and reduces the purchaser's confidence in the final numbers.

---

[2] I know I said to show profit, but don't do it like this. A savvy buyer or lender will see this and recast the financials anyway. Grow your business and monitor your expenses and only write off true expenses and show profit the old-fashioned way: earn it.

Every item that has to be 'recast' slows down the velocity of the transaction and makes the buyer or lender less confident in the determined value.

In addition, should the purchase price include third-party debt, the lender is unlikely to put up with significantly recast financials. Banks like certainty and dislike uncertainty.

Your goal should be to keep your financials as clean as possible. This will increase certainty and make the process go faster – something we call "velocity." Velocity is the speed of the transaction from the initial demonstration of interest to the closing. It is not only a consideration of the total time the transaction takes, but also the idea that the transaction is consistently moving forward toward closing. Delays in the transaction – like the purchaser waiting for the documents it has requested to be provided by the seller, or waiting for accountants to finish reviewing financials, or waiting on attorneys to finish drafting documents – reduce the likelihood a transaction will close. Once you have interest and a willing buyer and a willing seller, getting through legal and accounting and lending due diligence as quickly as possible and demonstrating constant forward motion is essential. Shoddy record keeping and poor financials are often causes for deal-killing delay.

A Tale of Two Businesses

Let's look at two companies' net profits and see how showing a profit every year will make a company more valuable and easier to finance and sell. Both of these business were equally profitable over five years, showing $5 million in net profit over the period, as so:

Company 1: Net Profits:

Year 1: $450,000
Year 2: ($100,000)
Year 3: 2,500,000
Year 4: ($200,000)
Year 5: $2,350,000
Total: $5,000,000

Company 2: Net Profits:

Year 1: $450,000
Year 2: $800,000
Year 3: $950,000
Year 4: $1,300,000
Year 5: $1,500,000
Total: $5,000,000

Which is more valuable?

Which is easier to sell?

The first, with its ups and downs, is unpredictable. Risky. The losses, and the sudden increases, will require explanation. Explanations slow deals down, increase risk, and therefore lower value.

The second company shows steady growth over time. Reliable profitability. Less risk. Fewer explanations. Greater value.

Now consider Company 3:

Company 3: Net Profits:

Year 1: $0
Year 2: $0
Year 3: $0
Year 4: $0
Year 5: $0
Total: $0

What is this company worth?

At first glance, the answer is $0.

There will have to be explanations. "We zeroed out the books every year to reduce taxes" is the explanation one always hears.

OK, but how much would the company have made?

The profit and loss statements will be recast. The money you wroteoff for your son's band will be returned to profits. The fact that you basically lived off company credit cards and wrote off all the payments will be explained. But the extent of these retconned profits will be somewhat conjectural – and therefore riskier.

More risks equal fewer turns on the net profits in the final valuation.

The process of creating and then explaining the recast financials will take time and cost important deal velocity. Even if the recast financials ultimately show the same net profits as Company 2, Company 3 will not be as valuable.

Slower deals reduce confidence in the final numbers and equal fewer turns on the net profits in the final valuation.

The doubt and risk introduced by having to substantially recast the financials will have a price.

Conclusion: To begin to build business value now, show a healthy annual net profit, and, over time, grow that net profit to a figure that will support the valuation you seek, while minimizing transactions that will have to be recast or explained.

Two

Focus on Revenues
Show Top Line Growth Over Time

It isn't all about the bottom line – the top line matters, too. Buyers will want to see a consistent gross revenue increase over time. You can't get comfortable – if you want to sell eventually, you must continually grow those revenues.

It is not hard to have a steep growth curve during your startup and ramp-up phases --- the first three to five years of your business. But after that many small business owners become complacent about gross revenue. The business is doing fine, they are making a decent enough living, and the focus tends to be on maintaining the status quo or growing profits by cutting expenses and streamlining operations.

> *While profit is the measure small business owners tend to focus on, having a long--term growth curve tells a great story about your business and will go a long way to attracting a buyer.*

A buyer is likely to be using a significant portion of your business's cash flow to pay you or repay his lender or his 401(k) over the first three to seven years he operates the business. A profitable company with a flat growth curve means that if the buyer wants to make any significant money during that time, he will have to change things up and figure out a way to grow the business.

But if you can show a long--term steady growth curve, you are selling him not only your profitable business but also the way for him to grow the business and therefore have money during the buy-out period. This makes your company easier to sell.

Buyers want to buy a growing company.

Track Top-Line Revenue Thoughtfully

How you track top-line revenue matters as well. Buying a business is all about assessing value and the risk to that value. How a buyer (or lender) looks at risk may be different for different buyers and different industries, but there are commonalities. Some assess risk by the concentration of revenues among product or service lines, or among customers. Some assess risk based on recurring revenue and customer loyalty.

It is worth some time in your strategic planning sessions to consider how a buyer or lender may assess risk in your industry, and then to make sure you track gross revenue in that way. For example:

- A law firm may want to be able to track top-line revenue generated by each attorney, so they can assess when revenue becomes too concentrated in a few professionals.

- A SAAS provider may want to track recurring revenue separately from project revenue, to assess the percentage of expenses covered by recurring revenue (and set goals around that), and to show stickiness and growth of recurring revenue over time.

- A service provider may want to track revenue by customer, to assess when it is becoming too reliant on a small number of customers and set goals to diversify and lower risk.

- A product company may want to track revenue by product line, as well as the cost of goods by product line, so it can assess profitability among lines and weed out bad products and show diversification.

This tracking can be done, depending on your accounting software, by creating sub accounts of revenue or adding tags or such. You will want to be able to look at gross revenue as a whole, and then also see it broken down in ways that make sense for your business.

There are other good reasons to track top-line revenue in thoughtful ways. By organizing your top-line revenues by different product or service offerings, you can see what percentage of your total revenues is coming from each. This can help you avoid overconcentration in one offering and spread risk.

You should also track costs of sales or costs of goods sold for each category of revenue you are tracking. The costs of sales or costs of goods sold should be costs that you only incur if you sell that product or service. This separates those costs from your general overhead, which you should track in expenses. Have a separate "costs of sales" or "costs of goods sold" category for each separate revenue category you are tracking. This allows you to see the margin for each product or service. For example:

Revenue

In-Person Training	$100,000
Content Creation	$200,000
Online Training	$50,000
Coaching	$100,000
Total Revenue	$450,000

Costs of Sales

In Person Training COS	$50,000
Content Creation COS	$75,000
Online Training COS	$10,000
Coaching COS	$75,000
Total COS	$210,000

If you are only tracking totals, you can see that your overall margin is 53% - under Revenue, you make $0.53 for every $1.00. But by looking at each category separately, you can see that your margins are different across different offerings: 50% for In-

Person training, 63% for Content Creation, 80% for Online Training, and 25% for Coaching. This tells you where you might want to focus your business development efforts: more on Content Creation and Online Training, less on Coaching.

Knowing your margins helps you plan, because it also gives you a clearer view of your total overhead.

Your Expenses, shed of the true Costs of Sales, represent the amount you must make every month to pay all your normal bills. Knowing this amount (some people call it your "nut") and knowing your margins ((100-(COS/Rev)) can show you quickly whether you are profitable, and can highlight the quickest ways to grow your way to success.

Conclusion: Focus on increasing your top-line revenue, year after year. You will find that it doesn't take much more than what you are otherwise doing to run your company, or certainly what you did to grow the company in the first place. It mostly just takes intentionality. You can also consider adding other product lines or services to your offerings to increase gross revenues. Customize your chart of accounts to track gross revenue and costs of goods or services by subcategories that make sense in your industry - with an eye to demonstrating low risk.

Keep Good Corporate Records

Corporate Secretary Adds Value

Whether you will eventually sell assets or your company as a whole, the buyer will be buying from you currently. Most likely you own either a limited liability company or corporation.

> Make sure you have all your corporate records in good shape early.

Most businesses will start with some contractual relationships — with suppliers or vendors or customers or landlords or tenants or contractors or employees or even with lawyers. Someone in your organization needs to have all of your contracts organized, available and kept up to date and needs to make sure they are renewed when they expire. I like to call this person the Corporate Secretary.* Most businesses need one (either full time or as a part of someone's time).

The primary responsibility of the Corporate Secretary is to ensure that Board members have the proper advice and resources for discharging their fiduciary duties to the

---

* A "Corporate Secretary" is an officer of a business corporation. Most states require corporations to have at least three officers: a President, a Treasurer, and a Secretary.

** The original meaning of secretary was one who can keep a secret.

Three

Keep Good Corporate Records
A Corporate Secretary Adds Value

Whether you will eventually sell assets or your company as a whole, the buyer will be buying from your entity. Most likely, you own either a limited liability company or a corporation.

> *Make sure you have all your corporate records in good shape early.*

Most businesses will start with some contractual relationships – with suppliers or vendors or customers or landlords or tenants or contractors or employees or even with owners. Someone in your organization needs to have all of your contracts organized, available, and kept up to date, and needs to make sure they are renewed when they expire. I like to call this person the Corporate Secretary[3]. Most businesses need one (either full time or as a part of someone's duties).

The primary responsibility of the Corporate Secretary[4] is to ensure that Board members have the proper advice and resources for discharging their fiduciary duties to the

---

[3] A "Corporate Secretary" is an officer of a business corporation. Most states require corporations to have at least three officers: a President, a Treasurer, and a Secretary.

[4] The original meaning of 'secretary' was 'one who can keep a secret'.

shareholders. The Corporate Secretary is also responsible for ensuring that the minutes of each Board meeting reflect the proper exercise of those fiduciary duties.

The Corporate Secretary is also a confidante and resource to the Board and senior management, providing advice on Board responsibilities and logistics. The Corporate Secretary is a senior, strategic-level corporate officer who plays a leading role in the company's corporate governance.

What are the Corporate Secretary's Specific Roles and Responsibilities?

- **Corporate Record Keeping:** The Secretary maintains a current record of key corporate documents, including bylaws, meeting minutes and records of actions, shareholder records, records of required state corporation and regulatory filings, and key contracts.

- **Corporate Filings:** The Secretary is responsible for ensuring the Corporation is current on state corporation law and regulatory filings.

- **Board and Shareholder Meetings:** The Secretary manages all Board and shareholder meeting logistics, ensures proper notices have been sent, attends and records the minutes of all Board and shareholder meetings, advises the Board on its roles and responsibilities, facilitates the orientation of new directors and assists in director training and development.

- **Stock Records:** The Secretary oversees the logistics of stock issuance and transfer, including the issuance and cancellation of share certificates and keeping the shareholder records up to date.

Do small businesses need a Corporate Secretary?

All corporations must have a corporate secretary. Often, in small businesses, the attorney appoints one of the founders as Secretary and that person never knows what they are supposed to do or does any of it. The first sign that a small business should have had an active corporate secretary is when the corporation is sued and cannot produce the required business records to show it was not merely the alter ego of its founders, or when a regulatory filing is not made, or when there is a lawsuit between the partners and the records are out of date and do not reflect the reality of how the company was governed.

In other words, the owners discover that they need a Corporate Secretary when it is too late, and that can be an expensive mistake.

If the business has shareholders that are not active employees or managers of the corporation, an active Corporate Secretary is imperative. If the business is a business partnership that has more than one owner/manager, then having an active Corporate Secretary is imperative. If the business is in an industry where there are numerous regulatory filings to track, such as the requirement to file annual reports in several states or to file annual or biannual licensing renewal, then having an active Corporate Secretary is imperative. The only corporation that can reasonably afford to do without an active Corporate Secretary is a solo entrepreneur operating in just one or two states in a business with few regulatory hassles.

What about LLCs?

There is no required office of "Secretary" in a limited liability company, and LLCs generally have more relaxed record keeping and reporting requirements than corporations. However, if your business LLC has members who are not active in the business, or has multiple members, or is in an industry where there are numerous regulatory filings to track, then it is a good idea to create a Company Secretary position. Of course, if you want to build business value, then a Corporate Secretary keeping good records can be a value multiplier.

Does the Secretary need to be full time?

The Secretary needs to be able to devote as much time to record keeping and governance as your company needs. Active Corporate Secretaries can also play key roles in staying abreast of and recommending new governance 'best practices' to the management team and Board, and can help the Board keep their focus on long term strategy rather than getting too focused on near term imperatives. That being said, for many small businesses, Corporate Secretary is not a full time position. The solution is either to make one of your full time partners or employees also the Secretary, or to hire an outsourced Corporate Secretary. Should you decide to stay in-house, the key is to make sure the person selected has the knowledge and skills to do the job, and has the time to devote to it, so that the required record keeping is not overlooked while the person focuses on their primary responsibility.

Should our lawyer be our Corporate Secretary?

A legal background is not required to carry out the duties of the Corporate Secretary. The corporation's attorneys are responsible for giving the company legal advice. The Corporate Secretary is responsible for giving the company governance advice. In fact, having a Corporate Secretary who also provides legal advice creates difficult questions about whether a particular communication made to management is legal advice - which may be subject to the attorney-client privilege – or general corporate/business advice, which is not. If your lawyer is your Corporate Secretary, this may make some of your communications with that lawyer non-privileged and that can be a surprise to everyone.

The "dual hat" corporate secretary/lawyer must always be careful to distinguish (and, as secretary, record) which "hat" is being worn, and whether it is legal or governance advice that is being given. If there is litigation between the partners or between management and non-managing shareholders in the future, you can be sure that the dual role will become litigated, the lawyer is likely to be disqualified, and the entire mess will be expensive.

The corporate lawyer has a key role to play in the life of the corporation, even a small business corporation.

The lawyer must help to train the Corporate Secretary and help the Corporate Secretary to identify the line between governance advice and legal advice, so that the Corporate Secretary does not unwittingly engage in the unauthorized practice of law.

Business Value

When you decide to sell your business, the buyer will engage in a period of due diligence, where they ask to see the various business and accounting records of the company, in order to verify the accuracy of the financial statements and tax returns and to assess the risk that the business will continue to perform in the same manner after acquisition.

One key element to a potential sale transaction is velocity. Once you have an interested and qualified purchaser ready to move forward, the more quickly you can deliver due diligence items that are clear and look good, the better. Let's say I am interested in buying your business, and your financials look good. You have strong and growing top and bottom line revenues. I want to be sure the company can continue to make the same or better revenues and profits after I buy it, so I ask you for your contracts.

Why do I want the contracts? I want to ensure that the contracts themselves bear out the production numbers and revenues I see on the financials. I want to make sure the contracts are current, and not expired – if you are doing business with old friends of yours on a handshake, then there is a lot of risk that those deals will disappear or change after I buy the business. I want to make sure the contracts are assignable, or what the assignment process is, and that they do not terminate on a "change of control" in the business. This is especially common in lending agreements, and if your company has debt I'm wanting to assume, that is a critical point.

Now, let's assume that, in answer to my request to see the contracts, you say "I'll get those together" and then it takes days, or weeks, or months. When the contracts finally are delivered, some are missing, some lack signatures, others are expired. I think you can see how this would erode confidence in the buyer that they are buying a business that has been well run and can continue to achieve results after the sale.

In contrast, if the seller immediately delivers a spreadsheet that has all the current contracts, organized by type and date and party, with expiration dates, and has an electronic database of all the current contracts, signed, you can see how this gives the impression of organization and competence and makes the buyer feel less risk.

Conclusion: Corporate Secretary, or Company Secretary in an LLC, is a key role that requires someone with the training, and the time, to perform it well. Read any account of the causes of expensive business litigation and you will find poor record keeping, especially of ownership and governance records, to be cited as one of the most common factors leading to protracted lawsuits. Good records allow cases to settle more quickly. Poor record keeping can also be the cause of a corporation's shareholders losing their limited liability, or of a company losing its regulatory authority or state licensure to do business. Poor record keeping distracts the Board from long term planning and causes the boards to lose their focus and their institutional memories. Good record keeping adds value to the business by allowing it to conduct due diligence with velocity and to reassure a buyer that the company has been operated well. A good Corporate Secretary (full time or part time) is an asset to your business.

Four

Protect Intellectual Property
Register Your Trademarks and Copyrights

All   businesses   have
intellectual property

All businesses have intellectual property, even if it's just a common law trademark for their name or slogan. You may also have copyrights or patents. Act early to actually file for formal registration of all your intellectual property.

It is important for entrepreneurs to protect their new business's intellectual property – hopefully before they launch. Not all companies will have a patent, and many will not have a protectable copyright. Every small business, though, sells their product or service using a brand name, and most have a logo or tagline. These brand names, logos, and taglines are the business's trademarks. You can protect these trademarks by registering them with the United States Patent and Trademark Office (USPTO).

Trademarks

Registration will protect the trademark (no one can make you stop using the mark) and will allow you to stop others from using confusingly similar names and logos to sell a competing good or service. Selecting protectable names and logos and going about protecting them by registering the trademark at the USPTO is critical. Here's how:

1. Select a Good Name: The first step to protecting your trademark brand name is to select a name that can be protected. Not all brand names can be protected. More importantly, even where a brand name has been registered, it may be so weak that enforcing the registration in court would be impossible or expensive.

What makes a good, strong, registrable trademark?

- **Suggestive Names:** Suggestive names 'suggest' something about the good or service. "DAYTIMER" for a personal calendar is suggestive of a quality of a product without generically describing the product.

- **Fanciful Names:** Fanciful names are made-up words with no dictionary meaning. "QUIZNOS" and "CISCO" are fanciful names. Many fanciful names, like "Goodyear" or "MicroSoft," are combinations of chunks of real words into a new, suggestive work. These trademarks combine the fanciful with the suggestive.

- **Arbitrary Names:** Arbitrary names are real words that have no association with the product or service. "APPLE" has nothing to do with computers. "BLACKBERRY" has nothing to do with cell phones.

Both are real words but are used arbitrarily as strong trademarks.

2. Conduct a Trademark Search: The next step is to conduct a trademark search using the USPTO Trademark Database. This search will show whether the trademarks you are considering are worth the trouble of attempting to register or whether you should go back to the drawing board. If your selected trade name is not registerable, you should carefully consider whether you want to spend the time and money to promote a brand that you cannot protect. Here are a few things to keep in mind about registrable trademarks:

- First, your brand name must not be 'confusingly similar' to an already registered trademark for the same or a similar product or service. If your mark is similar to another company's brand, and you are selling related goods or services, your trademark is weak or even not registrable.
- Surnames are weak or unregistrable.
- Brand names that are merely descriptive or geographically descriptive are weak or unregistrable. If you sell bicycles, you can't register the trademark "Bicycle Store" and then hope to stop other sellers of bicycles from using that name. Misspellings of descriptive or generic wording are also likely to be rejected.

- Deceptive, disparaging or offensive brand names will also be rejected.
- Of course, you can't register (or use) some other person's (or famous character's) name or likeness without their permission.

3. Determine Your Class of Goods and Services and Identify Your Goods or Services: A trademark is the brand name you use to sell a *specific* good or service. When you register to protect your trademark, you must select the class or classes of goods or services you are marketing with the trademark. The USPTO uses the International Schedule of Classes of Goods and Services to separate trademarks into classes. You can use your trademark to sell goods or services in more than one class, but you must pay a separate filing fee for each class in which you register. In addition to selecting a class, you must also clearly and precisely identify the specific goods or services you are selling. Examples of acceptable descriptions can be found in the Acceptable Identification of Goods and Services Manual.

4. Obtain Acceptable Proof of Use in Commerce: You cannot register your trademark until the trademark has been used to market and sell the product or service in interstate commerce. In order to register the trademark, you must submit acceptable proof of the trademark's use. Proof of use for products shows the trademark as used on the actual product - a label, packaging, or product display. Don't submit advertising material, press releases, invoices, etc. Proof of use for services shows the trademark as it is used in the sale or advertising of the services. Advertising, brochures, business cards and letterhead that refer to the services, and photographs of business signage are all acceptable for services. Note that you can file for trademark protection for your trademark before you begin to use the trademark in commerce by filing an "Intent to Use" application. An "Intent to Use" filing reserves the mark for a temporary period and must be followed up by filing a separate proof of use before the reservation period expires. Only after the proof of use is filed and accepted is your trademark registered.

5. File for Registration: You file your application to register the trademark online at the USPTO. Federal registration of your trademark gives you several advantages:

- Provides notice of your claim to the trademark. Not only is this notice important in legal proceedings, it also may prevent others from even attempting to use a similar trademark because they will find your trademark when they search the USPTO database.

- Legal presumption of ownership nationwide. If you do get into a dispute, your registration gives you the upper hand.

- Exclusive right to use the mark on or in connection with the goods/services listed in the registration. Not only can others not stop you using your registered mark, you can use the power of the federal courts to stop others from infringing on your trademark.

- Register with Customs. You can register your mark with US Customs to prevent infringing products from being imported.

- Consider a trademark lawyer. You are not required to use a lawyer to file your trademark application, but it's a good idea. There are many nuances to the registration process, from determining whether your name is registrable to properly identifying the class, good and service and writing an identification that will protect you. Dealing with the Trademark Examiner and their almost inevitable concerns and changes can also be tricky. Hiring an experienced trademark lawyer is usually money well spent. The lawyer can also help you navigate licensing and enforcement issues once the trademark has been issued.

What happens next? A month or so after you have applied for registration, you will receive an Office Action telling you what changes need to be made to your application. Maybe the description of goods and services needs to be tweaked. Maybe some portion of your trade name is too generic and needs to be properly disclaimed. Maybe your electronic logo is not acceptable, or your proof of use is not good enough. Whatever – there's usually something. You will have a month or two to respond, and if you fix the problem (or if it's determined that there was no problem), the USPTO will publish the trademark in the Official Gazette. There is a 30-day opposition period after publication, during which time anyone who believes registration would harm them can oppose registration. If no one opposes your registration, you are registered. You get a lovely certificate for your Intellectual Property Portfolio, and you can begin to use the ® with your trademark. From there, you will need to file renewal statements at the six-year point and the ten-year point, and every ten years after that, showing you're still using the trademark.

Copyright

Copyrights protect original expressions reduced to a tangible form. We are all familiar with copyrights for books, but other tangible forms of expression are copyrightable as well. Original computer programs are a good example of a commonly copyrighted intellectual property.

Because there are different rules for copyrighting different forms of expression, I'm not going to run through the process as thoroughly as I did for trademarks. Copyrights, like trademarks, can be claimed informally - but for full protection they require a filing with the U.S. Copyright Office (see www.copyright.gov). There are different forms to be completed and different deposit requirements for the various types of copyrightable forms of expression, including literary works (fiction and nonfiction, articles, anything original you write), performing arts (music, sound recordings, etc.), visual arts (artwork, jewelry, architecture), digital content (computer programs, databases, blogs, websites), motion pictures (including videos), and photographs.

Business Value

Taking the steps to formally protect your trademarks, as well as any copyrights or patents you may have, will help build business value.

> *Not only do those filings provide protection for those assets, the act of filing for protection and receiving certificates gives your business value in the eye of a potential buyer.*

Any savvy buyer's due diligence items will include intellectual property review. If they see your trade name or slogan as having some value, but you have not protected it, then the value of that intellectual property is diminished. In fact, if their review reveals that you didn't protect your intellectual property and in fact there are filings by others that could render your intellectual property as potentially infringing, it could kill a deal altogether.

Conclusion: Few things are worse than pouring time and money into building your small business brand into something valuable and recognizable, only to get a cease and desist letter from a lawyer telling you that your trade name is infringing on their client's trademark and that you have to change your name. Or to have someone copy and unfairly use your computer program or video without attribution or royalty. Spend the time and money to register your trademarks, copyrights and patents before you market them. Doing so will protect your business and help build business value for the future.

Five

Enact Financial Controls

Trustworthy Financial Statements Are Imperative

Selling your business — whether to an insider or a third party — is likely to give banks or investors or even buyers who are going forward to review and rely on your financial statements. In fact, the financial statements will be the primary driver of the value you receive for your business. It isn't that the financial statements themselves create value; it is that the financial statements will be the primary tool everyone uses to evaluate the business.

> Financial Statements are the lens through which the operations and health of the business are viewed.

As we have discussed elsewhere, buying a business is all about applying an assessment of risk to the operations of the business — the more risk, the lower the value. Assessing risk can be hard, and a lot of that assessment occurs inside someone's head. The numbers tell a story, but if you trust the numbers heard before that having add-backs and other items in your financial statements will inherently cause buyers and investors and lenders to trust the numbers less, increasing the perceived risk.

Five

Enact Financial Controls
Trustworthy Financial Statements Are Imperative

Selling your business – whether to an insider or a third party – is likely to involve banks or investors or even buyers who are going to want to review and rely on your financial statements. In fact, the financial statements will be the primary driver of the value you receive for your business. It isn't that the financial statements themselves create value, it is that the financial statements will be the primary tool everyone uses to evaluate the business.

> *Financial Statements are the lenses through which the operations and health of the business are viewed.*

As we have discussed elsewhere, buying a business is all about applying an assessment of risk to the operations of the business – the more risk, the lower the value. Assessing risk can be hard, and a lot of that assessment occurs inside someone's head. The numbers tell a story, but do you trust the numbers? I said before that having add-backs and other items in your financial statements will inherently cause buyers and investors and lenders to trust the numbers less, increasing their perceived risk and lowering the overall valuation. So the obverse must also be true – if the numbers are trustworthy, risk is lowered and valuation solidifies.

How, then, does one add trustworthiness to the financial statements? Having a good financial controller or CFO inside the business who keeps good books and categorizes items correctly and clearly is a must-have baseline. But there are other steps you can take beyond that – steps you will want to take as you grow to add value.

Having a CPA do your taxes and prepare at least an annual tax basis financial statement is a good beginning. The CPA can help you categorize things properly, get your chart of accounts looking good, decide which items are properly costs of goods or costs of sales and which are expense items, create a good clean equity section, etc. It is best to start off on solid ground by engaging a good CPA at start-up. But just having a CPA do your taxes is not going to get you where you need to be for a valuable exit.

At some point you will want to start paying the CPA for reviewed financial statements. This is not inexpensive and it can be a lot of work for you, so it is not something you are likely to begin in start-up mode, unless your start-up is well-funded and has investors. With annual reviewed financials, the CPA firm doesn't merely take the accounting files you give them and make sure they look right, and give you adjustments to make for year-end items.

With reviewed financials the CPA will actually review the items on the financials and test those items against internal records.

They will want to see at least a sample of the contracts, invoices, promissory notes, etc. that are reflected on the financial records of the business. Gathering these items for them is a chore (made easier if you are keeping good records) and you have to pay them to review all these items, of course. But now a third party like a buyer or investor or lender can have more comfort that the items on the financial statement have been reviewed by your CPA firm and are more likely to be accurate. The numbers are more trustworthy. There is less risk.

The next step, and one which not everyone gets to, to be sure, is to have audited financials. Auditing is even more expensive than a review and consists of a second CPA firm (not the one who ordinarily does your taxes or your review) doing a more complete review of your financials and your operations. This will include both internal controls testing and reaching out to third parties (vendors, customers) to confirm the items on your financial statements. Audited financials become necessary for certain contracts, customers, lenders or purchasers. One cannot, however, simply go get audited financials – you already need to have proper financial controls in place to be tested, and these are difficult to implement overnight.

What is a financial control?

> *A control is a procedure put into place in order to mitigate some risk.*

Financial controls, then, are procedures you implement in order to control financial risks such as overpayment, underpayment, embezzlement, fraud, etc.

Implementing a control really has two parts: creating a procedure that must be followed in order to control the risk, and collecting evidence that the procedure is regularly followed in order to allow the auditor to test the control. Many people do the first ("yes, we have that policy") but fail at the second ("we can't prove we do it"). So, any control you put into place must have a means of monitoring and measurement.

Putting financial controls in place and collecting evidence of compliance is not something that has to wait until you are ready for audited financials. You can put these controls in place early on, even at start-up. Not only will they help prepare you for auditing later if you need it, but because you can demonstrate their effectiveness, they will also add additional credence to your financials in general. Even if they are internal or CPA reviewed, they may save you from the very risks they are intended to control.

Here are some basic financial controls you might consider implementing. Your CPA should be able to walk you through creating the proper procedure and documenting evidence for any of these:

1. Overall financial management and implementation
   - Qualifications for and employing only certified, qualified financial managers and staff.
   - An efficient, direct chain of communication among the accounting staff and senior-level managers.
   - Periodic training and information sessions for accounting staff.
   - Periodic financial analysis and evaluation of financial ratios and statements

2. Cash inflows
   - Credit policy for all customers before entering into a creditor-debtor relationship with them.
   - Periodic reconciliation of bank statements to the general ledger.
   - Periodic review with all existing credit customers to ensure ongoing creditworthiness.

- Support files and backups for all financial data in a separate secured database with access only permitted to senior management staff.

3. Cash outflows
   - Automatic/subscription payments to be monitored and requiring proper authorization.
   - Maintaining a vendor database with detailed purchase records with restricted access in order to monitor cash outflow efficiently.
   - Clear and precise expense reimbursement policy, including detailed expense reports and receipt verifications.

Of course, there are many, many more. AICPA SOC 1 is a set of financial controls that you can implement and have audited by an outside CPA firm in order to obtain certificated compliance with the SOC 1 standard. Unlike a full financial audit, the SOC 1 audit only tests your controls, but having such a certification would provide a lot of confidence that the controls were in place and functioning. This is less expensive than a full audit and in some cases may be a good step in between CPA reviewed financials and full annual financial audits.

Conclusion: Implementing financial controls will not only help protect your business from fraud or loss, it will also make your financial statements, whether internal, reviewed, or audited, more trustworthy and therefore reduce uncertainty and lower risk in the mind of a potential purchaser, investor, or lender. Controls can and should be added from the beginning, and more stringent controls can be added as the business grows. Your CPA can help you decide what controls to implement and when, and can help you decide how to properly gather evidence that the control is being used. This evidence-gathering is an essential part of having the control. Build business value now by implementing financial controls today, and review your controls annually to test whether they are being done, and to see if more controls should be added.

The Employees Are The Business

Attract and Retain Top Talent

Companies don't make things, sell things, or perform services—people do. If you want your business to have value, it must have good people. Nothing will sour a deal faster than the buyer getting the feeling that employees are unhappy, disgruntled or unproductive. Treat your team and the well and make sure key employees are not only happy and well compensated but also that you have "protected" the business with reasonable employment agreements.

Find, Train, and Keep Good Employees

Finding, training, and keeping good employees is really a corollary to protecting yourself. You cannot replace yourself without valuable and trusted employees. Not only will these employees create value by helping you grow your business, but they become a key asset in the sale that any future sold business additional strong value.

Before the key to all small business's personal relationships, you must have employees that foster those key relationships with your customers and suppliers, and with each other. Nothing compares more for the long term success of a small

Six

The Employees Are The Business
Attract and Retain Top Talent

Companies don't make things, sell things or perform services – people do. If you want your business to have value, it must have good people. Nothing will sour a deal faster than the buyer getting the feeling that employees are unhappy, disgruntled or unproductive. Treat your rank and file well and make sure key employees are not only happy and well compensated but also that you have protected the business with reasonable employment agreements.

> *Find, Train and Keep Good*
> *Employees.*

Finding, training and keeping good employees is really a corollary to replacing yourself - you cannot replace yourself without valuable and trusted employees. Not only will these employees create value by helping you grow your business, but they become a key asset in the sale that gives the sold business additional strong value.

Because the key to all small business is personal relationships, you must have employees that foster those key relationships with your customers and suppliers, and with each other. Nothing concerns me more for the long term success of a small business than when I walk in and see unmotivated employees doing a terrible job.

But how does one find good employees? HR Professionals write entire books and teach seminars on this issue, but the basics are to look for people that are competent, resourceful and engaged, and not necessarily in that order.

Competence is, of course, a must. But job task skills can be taught, and often I find I want to be the one to teach my employees how I want a task done. That being said, each job has basic skills the employee must come to the table with.

More important is resourcefulness. It can be difficult to determine this in an interview, but you sure can determine it in the first six months of employment.

Resourceful people solve problems, and when they run out of work, they find something to do that helps the organization - they don't go into "shut-down mode." You want a team full of resourceful employees, and it is hard, but not impossible, to teach this (easier with young people).

Finally, you need employees that are engaged. They understand what service the company provides its customers, and they are fully engaged in the mission of providing that service, even if that means staying a little late, or doing something that isn't strictly speaking "their job."

It is more difficult to teach engagement than it is to teach skills or even resourcefulness, but the way you lead and treat your workers can have a dramatic effect on their engagement in providing your company's service, even if it means doing a little more than their job requires of them. High engagement levels are not, however, an excuse to overwork or take advantage of your workers, or they will quickly disengage.

Once you find these capable, resourceful, engaged workers, you have to keep them, and to do that you have to create a work environment where everyone is treated with dignity and respect, so people like to work there. You also have to pay them what they are worth, and enough to live on, so that they are not resentful or distracted. Providing benefits can be a great help in this area, often providing more goodwill and peace of mind for your employee per dollar than a raise, and setting your company apart from your competitors in the competition for valued labor. Finally, when possible, give them incentives to make the business more profitable. For key senior employees, you should consider giving them a contract that removes them from the worry of employment at-will and in return commits them to the Company.

> *When you are ready to sell your business, these valuable employees are a great asset.*

Having them will help to convince the potential buyer that you are replaceable, and that there is a business to buy that exists apart from you. The buyer will likely want to come into the business and see the employees at work. If he sees these kinds of workers, the questions will be focused on how to retain them, and once negotiations begin to focus on retaining assets, you have built value and your bargaining position is strong.

Finally, if you have done a really excellent job of building business value by being profitable, showing revenue growth across time, building intellectual property, and other ways we will discuss, you've created the possibility that one or more of your key employees could obtain the financing to become your buyer, and that can be a great result.

Conclusion: Your employees are your business. Attracting and retaining great employees builds business value. The buyer will want to feel that they can keep the employees that are providing this value, and will want to see that they are happy with their work and loyal to the company. As a bonus, one (or all) of those employees could become your buyer!

Seven

Professionalize Management
Transition from entrepreneur to CEO

Most small businesses begin with the same effective organization chart – the entrepreneur as the hub of a wheel where every reporting spoke leads to and through the owner. You are involved in every decision, big and small. You know how much money is in the bank, how much you are owed and by whom, the details of your monthly expenses, and the status of every project. You know every customer and their wants and needs. You know the vendors. You are the business, and the business is you.

Typical Entrepreneur's Real Organization Chart

Of course, this is not sustainable. As the company grows, you begin to lose control. You start to feel overwhelmed. You can't keep everything in your head anymore. And you can't get anything done because everyone is calling you all the time to ask about everything.

> *If you are going to build a business that has value, you need to professionalize the management of the company. You need to get out of the middle and up to the top.*

But how?

First, know this is a process that could take some time. You will take small steps and only gradually will you be able to extricate yourself from that hub.

It begins with a new organization chart. First, create the chart of the company as it should be now (if you were at the top), with the people you have. Then create the chart as it will be in a year, and in two years. What positions are there? Who do you need? Should you add a salesperson? A project manager? A controller? More workers or supervisors? Think about your plan for the gross revenues the company will have at that time and ask what the company needs to look like in order to deliver that quantity of goods or services.

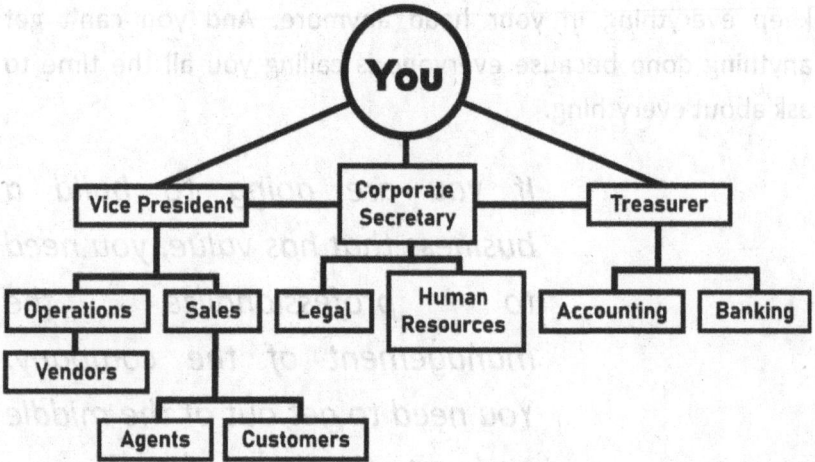

Professionalized Company Organization Chart

Next, make a hiring plan to grow the company to those levels. Who will you hire first? Who will train that person? When will you make the hire? On a predetermined date, or when a trigger event occurs, like signing a certain number of contracts or reaching a certain revenue target?

As you hire and train the new employees, consider creating an onboarding process to acclimate the new hires to your business and industry. Pay attention to reporting lines – and the fact that not all lines should go directly to you.

As manpower, and especially management, comes on board or is reorganized, begin to create documented processes and procedures for doing things. Professional companies rely on process and procedure to ensure successful operations. They rely less on continual heroic efforts to get things done.

Finally, treat the management team you have created like a small partnership. Have regular meetings and give them power in their respective spheres. Engage in strategic planning with the management team so that you all have a clear shared vision of the company's future. Get the group's commitment to the shared vision. Encourage open communication and insist on mutual unconditional positive regard, which becomes easier when everyone is committed to the same shared vision.

Most critically, insist on consensus. Once a decision is made by the management group, it must be enthusiastically adopted by the entire group as if it were their own decision. Encourage the managers to act in furtherance of this shared strategic vision, using the operational processes and procedures you have adopted. They should lead their teams within these parameters and report to you, but not upward delegate all decisions to you.

You will know this is working the first time someone reports a big success that happened without your involvement, or a big problem that was completely resolved without your intervention. Things will start happening – the company is becoming its own entity, separate from you.

In this step, you do retain a portfolio of important work to do. You should find that you have more freedom to think strategically and with the long-term in mind. You will be spending a good deal of your time managing the managers and installing and improving processes and procedures.

You also will retain some responsibility yourself. Maybe you are the face of the firm and still its best business developer. Or maybe you are the only one who can really develop that next, new product the company will launch. At this stage it is fine to retain that work – hopefully work you enjoy – but be allowed to delegate much of the other work of the business to trusted managers.

There will come a time when the professionalization is mature enough for you to take the next step and fire yourself.

The last step of professionalizing your management is to make the final transition from CEO to owner. You may not take this final step before you sell, but you should be prepared to. If you can demonstrate to a third party buyer that you have a successor CEO already trained and in your business, you open the door to potential buyers that want to buy a company, but not a job. If you are selling to a key employee, you need to be able to show that employee's bankers or backers that he is up to the task of filling your shoes. If you can't do this, be prepared for a buyer to demand that you stick around after the sale as an employee – exactly what you became an entrepreneur to avoid in the first place.

Replace Yourself.

When you offer your business for sale to that future buyer, the general idea is for you to go and do something else - retire, relax, start a new business, etc. But if you ARE the business, then how much value does the business have without you?

Entrepreneurs are generally highly motivated, strong performers. It is sometimes easier for them to do it all than to train people to do it for them. But if you want to have value for sale, the business needs to be able to operate and sustain itself with you out of the picture.

Entrepreneurs who fail this test often find their purchase offers conditioned on long-term employment or consulting agreements. This does not often work out well in the small business arena. The Seller continues to think of the company as his, and the new owners have a difficult time making the company theirs while the old owner is hanging around.

Buyers who see too much value in a selling entrepreneur's personal work in the company, but who aren't very excited about the seller hanging around, will also make an "earn-out" offer, where the final purchase price is substantially determined by the actual performance of the company after the sale. If the business is going to flounder when you're gone, your value is in real jeopardy.

Now, I realize that all business, especially small business, is at its core about personal relationships, and the key advantage a small business has over its large competitors is the ability of the entrepreneur to forge relationships with his customers. So, I am not advocating you become an absentee landlord. But you should train employees to perform the work of the business, while you focus on relationship building and strategy. When the buying entrepreneur steps in, the core business can continue to function, and the new entrepreneur will take over the relationship building.

Conclusion: An organization where you are in control of everything is not scalable. While it can be very difficult for an entrepreneur to give up control of all decision making and lean on others, you must move past that discomfort and slowly build a team you trust if you want to build business value. You must replace heroic efforts with processes and procedures and controls, replace micromanaging with reporting, and slowly remove yourself from the day to day and move up to the strategic level. If you can do this, your business can grow and build value beyond what you could have managed yourself.

Eight

Strategic Planning
Create a Shared Vision of the Company's Future

The most important thing you can do now to build a business with value is to regularly engage in rigorous strategic planning.

> *Your strategic plan will involve setting goals for the other recommendations in this book, as well as making sure everyone in the ownership and management team shares a common vision of the company's future.*

Often, I find that when members of a management team or partnership have heartfelt disagreements over important business decisions – and disagree to the point where they can't even understand each other's point of view – it is because they have different ideas of the ultimate goals and direction of the company. They both think they know where the company is headed, and they think everyone knows. But they actually have different visions of the future. This is because the team has not taken enough time to engage in strategic planning together and to create and commit to that shared vision that allows for better communication and unconditional positive regard for everyone's views.

To avoid this, take the ownership and management team offsite for a one- or two-day retreat for strategic planning no less than once a year, and as often as once a quarter. A one-day retreat must be focused and can be done more frequently. A two-day retreat builds in time for team building and bonding and the unstructured conversations that can be magical. How often you do either is up to you, so long as you do at least one per year.

How should you engage in strategic planning?

1. Plan to Plan

Strategic planning is a serious exercise that requires planning and commitment. Planning to plan is a key first step in the planning process.

First, you should decide who will attend the planning session. Start with the key management team. These are usually the direct reports to the owner. If you are at an early stage, everyone in the company may feel like a direct report to the owner, so ask yourself who the leaders are. Who will manage functions as the company grows? Who performs those key functions now? Of course, owners should all be present in most cases.

You may want a facilitator or management consultant to attend as well. Some people ask their outside accountant or lawyer to attend, but this can be expensive and can be limited to sessions where you may directly want their input. Some people like to include a secretary to make a good record of the meeting and decisions. This can be an administrative professional from your office who is discreet, or you can hire a temp just for this meeting.

2. Decide Where to Plan
Offsite is best. You want the team to be as free of daily work distractions as possible and away from the general staff (who may need to know the results but don't need to see the sausage being made).

For the first session, I recommend a two-day offsite retreat with everyone staying overnight and bonding over a meal together in the interim evening. After that, one-day sessions held two or three times a year or a two-day session once a year are fine.

Make sure the location has plenty of power, comfortable seating, and a white board or flipchart or screen to project a computer screen. The location should be comfortable, free of distractions, and a place where work can get done (like a big table everyone can sit around).

For the two-day retreats, a big Airbnb house with enough bedrooms for everyone can work well, or a hotel with rooms for everyone and a meeting space can work as well. For one-day sessions conference room rentals are ideal. Make sure there is coffee and drinks and snacks and generally plan to eliminate all the little things that people will worry over and get distracted from the work.

3. Decide When to Plan.
It can be hard to choose dates where all the key players will be free and able to attend. On regular workdays, they may feel they cannot leave work completely unattended by any management. On non-workdays (if you have those) there will be family time and events to contend with.[5] This planning is important, though, and deserves priority. Close for a day if you have to. Train up other employees to at least handle things for a day so you all can be away. Set the schedule to help (see below). But make the time to get this done.

4. Set the Agenda.
The content of your strategic planning sessions will change over time. Early in the company's life, you will begin by focusing on big issues like a vision statement or mission statement, development of the business's product and service offerings, deciding what your competitive advantage is (are you focusing on price, quality, or service?), looking at competition and perhaps a marketing plan. You will also take time to set the long-term exit strategy. An agenda will keep the meeting moving and give people an opportunity to get thoughts together before the meeting.

---

[5] Difficulty setting aside time can be a reason to choose a one-day over a two-day session, or vice-versa.

You can also build time into the schedule to allow managers to call back to the office and handle any important or urgent questions from staff. Take breaks between topics to allow people to stretch and refresh their minds. Take a lunch break but have lunch brought in if you can, so you don't break your rhythm too much. If you have planned a two-day retreat, make a plan for dinner (go out together or cook a meal together at the Airbnb). Limit day two to half a day and have lunch together before you head home.

On the agenda, identify who will lead each session, and who will take notes. The leader's job is not to present, it is to facilitate the discussion, ensure everyone is heard,[6] and build consensus. The leader should sum up conclusions clearly and set any action items and responsible parties. Each discussion topic should end with a decision and assigned actions – and the leader states those clearly so that the secretary can record them and so that anyone in the room who does not agree that the summation was accurate can speak up. The goal is to build a shared vision and consensus.

---

[6] This is one of the discussion leader's most important jobs. Even on a senior management team, there may be overwhelming people who tend to dominate discussions and more reticent people who will keep opinions to themselves unless directly asked. This can be the case even where everyone in the room is the same age, experience, title, race, sex, etc. and is even more likely where your team is diverse.

One person (like a consultant) can lead all sessions, or you can have different people lead each session. In general, I don't like the head owner or CEO to lead all the sessions – too much power at the front of the room stifles discussion and innovation. In fact, the owner or CEO should try to speak last and get the benefit of everyone else's ideas before weighing in, where possible.

5. Assign Homework.

Often, these planning sessions will involve finance, and so tasking the treasurer with bringing current financial statements is an example of homework that is often needed.

Depending on the topics to be discussed, you may have other homework to assign. Any data you predict the group will need to make decisions on any topic should be assigned to someone as homework. Sometimes, the homework will be presented by that person at the start of a topic, and sometimes they will just have the information prepared for reference during the discussions.

Often, during the discussion of a topic, the group will find it wants other information or data in order to make a decision. No worries – add that topic to the agenda for the next meeting, and make gathering that needed data homework for someone.

Typical Topics for Strategic Planning

Every strategic planning session I lead is different. The topics you choose will be driven by the stage of the business and the problems or opportunities it faces. Early-stage companies may face foundational issues like mission and vision statements, product lines, competitive advantage, and reporting and process. Mid-stage companies may need to focus on growth and transformation. Maybe you need to discuss acquisitions, or exit strategy, or the potential to launch a new product or service or enter into a new channel or market.

The possibilities are endless, but should be focused on long term goals and structural change, which should lead to a determination of operational next steps in order to investigate further, study, or implement the changes you have identified.

For example, perhaps you have identified a structural management problem with your employees and, after discussion, have decided that you need to implement a more thorough annual review system with goal setting, monitoring, and accountability. That is an excellent strategic goal. As the action item, you task the HR director with designing such a system for approval by the management team, and to having the design ready in 90 days. That is a good action item – it is specific, measurable, realistic and time-bound. That's all you need to do in a strategic planning setting. Actual system design and implementation are operational concerns, not strategic concerns, and you shouldn't allow them to bog you down during strategic planning time.

All that being said, there are a few exercises that make regular appearances in strategic planning sessions, and that can be done repeatedly (every year, every other year, etc.). Here is a brief outline of a few of those popular exercises:

Vision and Mission Statement

This is a great exercise for a start-up, and can be used by more mature businesses as well to refresh the vision and mission, especially when new products or services are added or a new long term strategy is adopted.

For this exercise it is important to understand the difference between the vision and the mission statement. They are not the same.

Your mission statement is focused on the company as it is now. The mission statement describes what we are doing right now, today, and every day. When you arrive at work, what are you about? What does the company do? For whom? Why?

For example, Amazon's Mission Statement is:

> We strive to offer our customers the lowest possible prices, the best available selection, and the utmost convenience.

And LinkedIn's:

> To connect the world's professionals to make them more productive and successful.

Uber:

> Uber's mission is to bring transportation — for everyone, everywhere.

For your mission statement, consider who you serve, what your value proposition is, whether your focus is on price, quality, or service, and what problem you're helping people solve. Keep it short – one sentence. I prefer Amazon's formulation – beginning the sentence with "We," because it brings home that the mission is a description of what we are doing.

Your mission statement makes an excellent beginning for an elevator pitch and can be shared with your entire workforce for everyone to have a short, agreed statement of what we are all about.

Vision statements are future-looking. Vision statements talk about what we will create together in the future. The vision is a glimpse of where we are headed. Let's look at the same companies:

Amazon's Vision:

> To be Earth's most customer-centric company, where customers can find and discover anything they might want to buy online.

And LinkedIn's:

> To create economic opportunity for every member of the global workforce.

Uber's:

> Smarter transportation with fewer cars and greater access. Transportation that's safer, cheaper, and more reliable; transportation that creates more job opportunities and higher incomes for drivers.

Vision statements are useful shortcuts in analyzing decisions, perhaps weeding out ideas before they come to a strategic planning session, or green lighting them for discussion. One can almost hear the conversations:

> "Does it help us create economic opportunities for some members of the global workforce? No? Then why would we do it?"

> "Does it make transportation safer, cheaper, or more reliable? Yes? OK let's discuss it at the next strategic planning session. I'll need you to bring data on how it does that and also the ideas' impact on job opportunity and income for our drivers."

I can't tell you how many times I have been at a networking event and met the owner or a key manager of a business and asked them what their company does, and been hit with a look of momentary panic, followed by a rambling answer that goes nowhere. Don't let this happen to you – get your vision and mission tight.

Exit Strategy

Are you building a company to sell to a third party? Are you planning to go public? Will the current owners exit through an ESOP? Will key managers buy out the founders at some point? When – five years? Ten? At what target valuation?

Importantly, does everyone on the team agree that this goal, in terms of time to goal and valuation, is achievable? It can be a stretch or a reach, but the goal shouldn't be completely unrealistic.

Keep in mind that all these answers can change over time. In fact, you can re-do this exercise every year if you like, changing the answer based on changes in circumstances. You don't need to be perfectly correct in your predictions, you just need a shared destination to steer toward. Most vehement disagreements among managers and owners occur because the team does not share a common vision of the destination. Discussing the plan, letting everyone participate, and putting the strategic plan on paper together will reveal areas where people are not in sync. Getting everyone to share and commit to a common vision and future decisions becomes easier.

*Setting the long-term exit goal
helps you set near term goals.*

Once you have set a long-term goal for the type of exit, the time frame, and the valuation, you can answer questions about what that company has to look like in terms of gross revenues and EBITDA. You will likely want to get some professional advice on this from a CPA or consultant, because these numbers will vary by industry. Keep in mind you don't have to be 100% right, you just need a common goal to aim for.

For example, if you decide that you want to sell this company to a third party in five years for $10 million, you can get information on what a company in your industry that sells for $10 million looks like. What EBITDA or gross revenues does it have? Does monthly recurring revenue drive the valuation? What other factors make a company in your industry that valuable? This is the critical second half of this Exit Strategy exercise – imagining the details of this company of the future.

Now, you can take this long-term goal and use it as a basis to set gross revenue and net profit targets for next year, and for the year after that. These will be based on a regular progression toward the long-term valuation goal over the period of time you have decided. Setting these revenue goals can lead to discussions about your current product and service offerings: can these grow enough to meet the goals? Or do you need to develop new or different offerings to meet the goals? This exercise dovetails perfectly with the Organization Chart exercise, which I detail later.

SWOT

In planning sessions I lead, I almost always include a SWOT discussion. SWOT stands for Strengths, Weaknesses, Opportunities, and Threats. People often get confused about the differences between Strengths and Opportunities, and between Weaknesses and Threats. The way I use them is to list current situations in the company as Strengths or Weaknesses, and future possibilities as Opportunities or Threats.

This is best done after goals are set, because you will want to discuss these items as they relate to your strategic goals.

You should start the SWOT session with simple brainstorming. Fill in each section, one at a time. Make sure everyone has an opportunity to add something to each section. If you have a reticent group or reticent people, you can even go in some order with each person adding something.

- What strengths does the company have that will help it meet the goal you set?
- What weaknesses do we have – what resources do we lack that are impeding our progress in implementing the plan?

- What opportunities are out there that we can take advantage of in order to follow the plan and achieve our goal?
- And finally, what threats to success exist?

Once all four quadrants are filled in, go back to Strengths and process the information you brainstormed, one quadrant at a time:

- How can we maximize or take advantage of those strengths?
- How can we overcome those weaknesses?
- What actions need to be taken to exploit those opportunities?
- How can we take steps to mitigate the threats or ensure we can recover if the threat materializes?

SWOT sessions leave everyone with a better understanding of the organization and its capabilities. You should leave the SWOT with some concrete ideas on exploiting opportunities and mitigating weaknesses. Again, this exercise can work well with the Organization Chart exercise.

Organization Chart

I tend to finish planning sessions with an organization chart exercise. One goal we have in growing business value is to professionalize management and work the founder out of a job. The organization chart is a key tool for accomplishing this. We also want to overcome any weaknesses in personnel we may have identified in our SWOT, and we want to build toward the company of the future we described in our Exit Strategy. Here is how I run this exercise:

The Organization Chart exercise begins by making a good chart that shows the organization of the business as it is today. Create the baseline. Often, I prefer to have the group build the current organization chart together by giving information to a scribe, who builds the chart on the screen or whiteboard as the group goes. You might be surprised that, even in small organizations, the senior management team does not share the same mental picture of how the business is organized – and that this can lead to some great "aha!" moments and even to conversations about how we should restructure the business as it is today. Let that happen. After a management team has been through this exercise once, though, you can start each subsequent time by handing out a current organization chart.

Next, build a second organization chart that shows what the company must look like three years from now, if you are to hit the revenue goals you agreed to earlier. For example, let's say you are doing $5 million a year in revenues now. You've decided as a group that your three-year plan is to have $10 million a year in revenue, and you all agree this is a realistic and achievable goal.

Now, build the organization chart the company will need in order to deliver twice the sales or services you are delivering today. This is a detailed version of the "Company of the Future" you may have created as a part of the Exit Strategy exercise, and it's limited to three years out because that is a realistic planning time frame. You may have set an Exit Strategy goal or five or ten years out to exit, but here we keep the event horizon tighter. In building this three years future organization chart, ask yourselves:

- Will you need more workers or service providers?
- More supervisors or managers?
- Additional sales or business development or marketing help?
- Will the controller who is also the human resources manager and the corporate secretary need to focus on one of those and hire people to do the other jobs?
- Will you be ready to add to top management – maybe add a COO or a CFO to the mix?
- Will you solve these problems by hiring experienced employees? By training and promoting? By outsourcing to independent service providers? By acquiring smaller businesses in the industry?

Add the employees you believe you will need to have in place in order to effectively deliver the goal level of product or service in three years. If you are going to rely on key third party vendors or contractors, I like to add them to the chart as well, with a reporting line to the person who is responsible to manage that asset (do you need to add someone who will manage those assets?).

The end result is the company you will be when you are meeting that goal. This is far more tangible than simply putting a number on the board.

As you build the future organization chart, keep in mind the SWOTs you have identified. Make sure you have built into the organizational chart the capabilities needed to meet those SWOTs. Here are some examples:

- You identified hacking as a serious potential threat, to be mitigated by creating a cybersecurity program. You should add to the future organization chart some cybersecurity capabilities. Perhaps you add an in-house Chief Information Security Officer, or perhaps you plan to hire an outside fractional CISO. Maybe you just want to add a third-party vendor to outsource to, but you'll need to hire or assign someone to manage them. Note these changes and additions on the organization chart.

- You are in the business of laying fiber optic cable for telecommunications, transportation, and defense companies. During strategic planning, you find that each team you have in the field can lay a certain amount of cable per year, at a certain revenue range and a certain profit range. Applying that analysis to the number of teams currently up and running shows that, in order to meet revenue goals, new teams must be added. Add these teams to the chart, along with the supervisors needed to manage them. Perhaps you also realize that with more teams, the operations manager can't manage safety too, and you add a full time Safety Manager to the chart as well.

- You operate a software company. When looking at weaknesses in your company as structured, you realize that the VP who is managing the data conversion process is also managing the customer service department and is spread thin. That VP can't continue to lead both effectively, especially if you double in size and add more data conversion work and additional service representatives. You decide that the existing VP is better suited to managing the data conversion process, and that it will be best to hire a new Customer Service manager. Add that role to the chart.

Once you have that chart built, the final part of the exercise is to make a plan for hiring for the next year.

Compare the two organizational charts and, keeping in mind your interim goals for this year and next year and your SWOT, decide what roles need to be filled immediately or as soon as possible. List those roles and prioritize them.

For some roles, you may decide to assign milestones that will tell you when you need to hire. If so, set clear triggers and set the processes in motion. For example, you may decide you have to add a new person in X role immediately, and a new person in Y role after sales hit $ZZZ per month.

For roles further out, you can set more general milestones (e.g., when we hit $6 million in revenue, we need to hire a new crew, and we need to hire a new crew for every million in revenue after that; or, once we add two new crews, we need to add another project manager) because you will have a chance to revisit those at next year's session.

Note that these discussions can also lead to thoughts about other resources needed to make the goal happen, like a larger facility/store or more equipment. Maybe you will need to buy more equipment as you add work crews. Maybe you will need a larger store as you add sales or want to expand to another location. This is all good and you can record those resources in the plan, along with the same kinds of milestones.

Conclusion: Regular and rigorous strategic planning is the secret sauce to building business value. All the other recommendations in this book can be considered and implemented with good strategic planning. When should we do it? How do we do it? What resources do we need in order to do it? These are the basic questions of strategic planning.

Strategic planning is how you develop goals and milestones. Then you create operational plans, processes, and procedures to implement the plan and train your employees to use those processes and procedures. Taking time for strategic planning keeps the management team from getting bogged down in the day to day operation of the business - keeps you from getting lost in the forest because you are only focused on the next tree. Building business value over time should be the overarching policy of the company. Use the strategic planning process to achieve that overarching policy.

Conclusion

Act Today to Build Value for the Future

Building a valuable company - one that someone else will buy from you for a multiple of the business's earnings - takes time. You simply cannot take all the steps necessary for a successful sale at the last minute. If you want to get the most out of the business when you sell it, you have to act now to create that value.

There are many ways to build a valuable business. This book gives you some of the most important steps to take, steps that are common across most business types and industries. Every one of these steps is within your power to implement, and every one of them will help to build value over time and will help to make that exit transaction go smoothly.

It goes without saying that there are operational steps your business must take as well. You need to be good at whatever it is you do and be able not only to deliver your product or service but also to market and sell that product or service. However, being good at what you do is not enough. You must also take the steps outlined here if you want to extract the value you have built.

I recommend you start with a strategic plan. Decide where you are headed, what your goals are. Then make a plan to implement each of these steps along the way. Having a plan will help you make the numerous small decisions you are called upon to make along the way, from how much profit to show at the end of each year, to whether to introduce a new product or service to increase gross sales, to hiring practices, whether to spend money on protecting your intellectual property, when to enact financial controls, and how to organize your team.

Then, revisit that plan at least annually. With your management team. Get out of the office and focus on the plan. Set new goals and milestones. Everyone on the team will be very busy on a daily basis paying attention to near term goals and challenges - take some time to intentionally get everyone to focus on the long term.

Good luck.

Appendix A

A Small Business Owner's Guide to Financial Statements

Financial Statements are records that present your business's financial activity in a clear and concise way. These records are used by a variety of people to review your business's financial health.

It is important for entrepreneurs to understand the different records that make up the financial statements and how they work. Properly used and understood, financial statements let you, the small business owner, understand and manage your own business more effectively, and help you present an accurate representation of the financial health of your business to important allies.

There are four documents that generally make up the financial statements of any business. They are:

- **The Income Statement** (also called the Profit and Loss Statement or the "P&L")
- **The Balance Sheet** (more formally the Statement of Financial Position)
- **The Statement of Cash Flows**
- **The Statement of Changes in Equity**

Each of these tells the story of your business in a different way. Taken together, they should offer the whole picture.

The Income Statement is used to look at the business's profitability. It measures and totals the business's income from all sources, and then shows the business's expenses. The final line of the Income Statement shows the business's net profit (or loss) over the period measured. The Income Statement covers a specific time period: monthly, quarterly, year-to-date and annual statements are the most common. You can determine the period covered in the income statement's title. An income statement entitled "for the month ended 3/31/XXX" covers all income and expenses incurred in the month of March. An income statement entitled "for the quarter ended 3/31/XXX" covers all income and expenses incurred from January 1 - March 31.

The Income Statement does not include money that may move in and out of the business that is not part of income or expenses. For example, if your business borrows money from someone during the period covered, that will not be shown on the income statement, because the money you get from borrowing is not "income" - it is not taxable. Similarly, if your business paid some of the principal of a loan back during the period covered, it will not be shown, because the repayment of a loan is not an "expense" - it is not deductible (the interest you pay on that loan, however, is an expense and is shown).

A final note about income statements: they may be prepared on a "cash" basis or an "accrual" basis.

Cash basis statements record items of income or expense as they are actually received or paid by the company. On a cash basis, you record income when you actually receive the money, and you record an expense when you actually write and send the check.

Accrual statements, on the other hand, record the items of income and expense when they are earned or incurred. On an accrual basis, you record income when it becomes owed to you (you complete the work and send the bill), and you record an expense when you owe the money (you receive the goods or the service), regardless of when you pay.

The Balance Sheet is used to show a business's assets, liabilities and equity at any given point in time. Balance sheets have a single date on them, and speak as of that day. Typically, one would present an Income Statement for a given period, along with a balance sheet for the last day of that period. An Income Statement "for the year ended 12/31/2014", then, might be accompanied by a Balance Sheet dated 12/31/2014.

The Balance Sheet measures all of the business's assets (cash, accounts receivable, inventory, equipment, property, etc.). Note that the balance sheet shows the depreciated value of those assets, and detailed balance sheets might even show the original basis (amount you paid, generally) of the item, and then show how much depreciation has been taken and show the net asset value (basis minus depreciation). All of the values of all of the assets are totaled as "Total Assets".

The Balance Sheet then measures liabilities (trade payables, the principal amount of debts or loans owed, taxes owed but not yet paid) and equity (the value of all shares in the company plus any retained earnings). The total of all liabilities and equity together must equal the total of assets. In other words, assets balances with liabilities plus equity. That is why it is called a "balance sheet," because it must balance. Any increase in a business's assets, without a corresponding increase in a company's liabilities, therefore increases the company's equity.

The Income Statement and the Balance Sheet are the two most commonly asked for and provided Financial Statements in a small business setting. The other two Financial Statements, though, are important to understand and can be used by the business owner to help better understand the business, even where they are not being asked for by outsiders.

The Statement of Cash Flows covers much of the same information as the Profit and Loss Statement. It covers items of income and expense for a certain period of time.

The Statement of Cash Flows has two important differences, however.

First, the Statement of Cash Flows is always a cash-basis statement. It measures the actual movement of cash in and out of the company. If the Income Statement was prepared on an accrual basis, the Statement of Cash Flows becomes critical to understand the company's actual cash position at any given time. For example, if your company is owed a lot of money it has not yet been paid, the Profit and Loss Statement (accrual basis) may show a healthy cash flow, when in fact the bank account is empty.

The Statement of Cash Flows will reveal the drought of cash and alert you to take action to get those bills collected, raise cash, or delay expenses.

The other important difference is that the Statement of Cash Flows includes movements of money that are not included on the Income Statement because they are not items of income or expense (receiving or paying loans, for example), and it does not include items that are on the Income Statement that do not involve actual movements of money (like depreciation expenses). In that way, the Statement of Cash Flows is a more accurate measure of the movement of cash and of your business's cash position even when the Income Statement was prepared on a cash basis.

Finally, the Statement of Changes in Equity looks specifically at the ways in which the "Equity" portion of the balance sheet changed over any given period. The Statement of Changes in Equity looks, like the Income Statement, at a given period of time, and measures the change in that portion of the balance sheet over that period of time.

Assume, for example, we had a balance sheet dated 1/1/2014, and another balance sheet dated 12/31/2014. Imagine also that the Equity portions of those two balance sheets (the Share Capital and the Retained Earnings) were different. Some change had occurred to the equity over the period. The Statement of Changes in Equity for the Year Ended 12/31/2014 would explain, in detail, the reasons for those changes. The Statement breaks down the reasons for the changes into categories (changes in accounting policy or corrections from a prior period, issuing or redemption of capital shares, income, etc.).

The Statement of Changes in Equity is most often used in a small business setting where there are non-managing investors who want an easy to review document that details what has happened with their investment, without having to wade through all the other Statements to figure that out.

Financial Statements can be used by business owners to better understand their business and its assets and cash flows, and to make decisions. Financial Statements are used by the business's professional advisers to make legal, business and tax/accounting recommendations. Financial Statements are used by investors to decide whether to invest in your business or to monitor their investment. Financial Statements are used by banks and other lenders to decide whether to make credit available to the business. The ability to understand and provide accurate financial statements can be critical for small business owners. In future posts, we will look at these important documents in more detail.

Appendix B

Basic Financial Terms and Analysis

A key part of managing your business is understanding your business's finances. Appendix A discussed the four basic financial statements, what they are and how they relate to one another. Here, I discuss some basic financial terms that every entrepreneur must know.

Balance Sheet Terms

Your balance sheet lists all of your business's assets, liabilities and equity on a particular date. To understand the balance sheet, you must understand:

Assets. Assets are all of the things with a monetary value that the company owns. Cash, securities, accounts receivable, inventory, land, buildings, vehicles, furniture, intellectual property, etc. Assets are generally things that can be sold to somebody else.

Liabilities. Liabilities are the debts of the company: money owed to suppliers (trade debt), debts owed to banks or other lenders (notes), accounts payable, taxes due. Anything the company owes to someone else that must be repaid is a liability.

Equity. Equity is the net asset value of the company to its owners at any point in time. Equity reflects the amounts the owners have put into the company (unless an owner made a loan to the company, which is a liability), plus retained earnings, or minus retained losses. On a balance sheet, the Assets always equal the Liabilities plus the Equity. That's how the balance sheet 'balances.' To calculate your company's Equity, then, you subtract the Company's Liabilities from its Assets.

Debt to Equity Ratio. Your company's debt to equity ratio is calculated by dividing the Liabilities by the Equity.

A company with $1,000,000 in Assets, $750,000 in Liabilities and $250,000 in Equity (remember, Assets = Liabilities + Equity) has a debt to equity ratio of 300% (meaning that creditors are providing three times more to the company than the shareholders). Lenders and investors care about the debt to equity ratio – the more debt you have in comparison to your equity, the less likely you are to attract a lender or investor.

A related term is the Debt Ratio, which measures Liabilities divided by Assets. Companies with debt that generate profits that exceed the cost of the debt will see their assets increase faster than their liabilities, which increases Equity. If you are generating profits below your costs of borrowing, you will gradually decrease Equity as Liabilities grow in comparison to Assets. Looking at the Debt Ratio over time - say by comparing a balance sheet dated 1/1/XXXX with a balance sheet dated 12/31/XXXX – will quickly tell you whether profits are greater than the costs of borrowing.

Fixed and Variable Cost. A variable cost is a cost that changes depending on the number of goods your company produces or the amount of products or services your company sells. A fixed cost is a cost you pay regardless of the number of goods sold or services performed.

Raw materials used in making your product, direct labor (labor costs you only incur in making a sale, like an hourly rate job that you service by paying a subcontractor by the hour), shipping costs, and sales commissions are examples of variable costs.

Rent on your building, the President's salary, and your internet bill are examples of fixed costs.

Profit and Loss Statement Terms.

The profit and loss statement (also known as the P&L, or sometimes as the Income Statement) lists your company's sales and expenses over a defined period (a month, a quarter, a year) and is used to work out the gross and net profit of a business. To understand a P&L, you must understand:

Sales. The money your company receives in exchange for its goods or services, also called Revenue. On a cash basis P&L, this is money your company has actually received. On an accrual basis financial statement, the sale happens and the revenue is booked when the goods or services are delivered, whether or not there is immediate payment.

Costs of Sales (also called Cost of Goods Sold). This is the cost of the raw materials and assembly of what your company sells, or the cost of the finished goods your company resells, or the direct costs of delivering the services your company delivers. This is what a manufacturing company pays for raw materials, what a bookstore pays the distributor for the book they sell, what a construction company pays a laborer for providing direct labor on a project, or a law firm pays an associate or paralegal for work on a client's legal matter. Costs of Sales are the variable costs incurred only if a sale is made, rather than the fixed costs (rent, administrative salaries, interest payments) your company incurs whether a sale was made or not.

Gross Profit (also called, confusingly, Net Revenue). This is simply Sales – Costs of Sales. It is the profit the company has after paying its direct costs of sales, but before paying any expenses.

Operating Expenses. Office rent, administrative and marketing and development payroll, telephone bills, Internet access, all those things a business pays for but doesn't resell. Taxes and interest are also expenses. Expenses include non-cash items, such as depreciation and amortization, but do not include payments that are not deductible from income, like dividends to shareholders or the repayment of the principal amount of a loan.

Break Even Analysis. Possibly the most important calculation the beginning entrepreneur will make is the break-even analysis. To make the break-even analysis, you must have a good handle on your fixed costs versus your variable costs. The break even analysis tells you what Gross Sales you must generate in order for your Net Profit to equal zero. In other words, how much revenue do you need to break even?

To calculate the break-even point, you have to first identify your variable expenses, and then calculate a cost per unit ratio: this is the average percentage of costs of sales per dollar of revenue. If you are a game store that resells games you purchase from distributors, and you generally mark your product up 100%, and you don't pay commissions or have any other direct costs of sales, then your cost per unit is $.50/$1.00. In other words, you make fifty cents Net Profit for every dollar of revenue.

Next, you must calculate your total fixed costs: how much you pay each month (quarter, year) in fixed expenses that do not vary based on sales. Rent. Salaries. Utilities. Insurance. This number is critical for your business, and you should not only try your best to calculate it before you open, you also should be refining it as you go.

Finally, divide the total of your fixed costs by the Net Profit per dollar, and you will determine break-even revenue. (Break Even Revenue = Fixed Costs/Net Profit per Dollar).

For example: If our game store has $10,000 per month in fixed costs, and earns $.50 per dollar in Net Revenue, the store's break-even point is $20,000 per month in gross sales.

Profits (and Losses). The "bottom line" of the Profit and Loss Statement is the Net Profit or Loss. Simply put, this is your total Sales minus Cost of Sales minus Expenses. If someone asks you, "what's your bottom line," this is your answer.

As an entrepreneur, you don't need to be an accountant (although you should have an accountant). You must, however, understand basic finance and be able to talk intelligently to shareholders, creditors, lenders, board members, and business partners about your company's financial health. You must also be familiar with the basic financial tools you can use to measure and monitor your company's financial help. Knowing these terms is a good start.

Acknowledgments

I have learned a lot about building business value from many people over the years.

I've especially benefited from the wisdom of long- time customers like Brad Cunningham, Ramon Ashy, David Peeples, and Bret Mingo.

My thinking has benefited greatly from numerous discussions about business with trusted advisors Phil Yanov and Richard Bliss, and from trying ideas out on new customers like the awesome folks at 10X Consulting.

I would like to thank my MasterMind group for their encouragement and accountability.

Thank you to Jennifer Oladipo and her team at Jenno Co. for providing their copywriting expertise.

Finally, thanks to my son Henry, who designed the graphics and cover art, and to my daughter Claire, for lending her editing and publishing expertise.

Author's Note

I hope you found this book to be useful. If you want to continue the conversation, you can:

Join my Mailing List by visiting me at www.fscottp.com and signing up. The newsletter has helpful tips for building business value and will keep you informed of other events and opportunities to engage.

Want more help? You can sign up for a one- or two-day Strategy Planning Session, led by me! I encourage businesses to engage in regular strategy planning, and I lead planning sessions for management teams. Visit www.fscottp.com/services to learn more.

Interested in a more regular conversation? I lead Build Value MasterMind Groups, with Phil Yanov. These Mastermind groups bring together business owners who are on a mission to build value in their business. The groups meet regularly as we build value and tackle the problems of growing business.

Connect with me on LinkedIn, or listen to more of my musings about business and living the entrepreneurial life on the Tech After Five Podcast, Connecting Better, with Phil Yanov. It's available wherever you listen to podcasts including your smart speaker.

Finally, if you enjoyed this book, help others find it by giving it a 5-star rating and a nice review on Amazon or Goodreads.

Thank you all.

-Scott

* 9 7 8 1 7 3 6 8 4 6 2 4 7 *